Classic Spot Illustrations

from the Twenties and Thirties

by James Montgomery Flagg,
Gluyas Williams, John Held, Jr. and Others

Edited by Herb Galewitz

Arranged by Carol Belanger Grafton

DOVER PUBLICATIONS, INC.
Mineola, New York

Bibliographical Note

Classic Spot Illustrations from the Twenties and Thirties: By James Montgomery Flagg, Gluyas Williams, John Held, Jr. and Others is a new work, first published by Dover Publications, Inc., in 2000.

DOVER *Pictorial Archive* SERIES

Library of Congress Cataloging-in-Publication Data

Flagg, James Montgomery, 1877–1960.
    Classic spot illustrations from the twenties and thirties / by James Montgomery Flagg
    . . . [et al.] ; edited by Herb Galewitz ; arranged by Carol Belanger Grafton.
        p. cm. — (Dover pictorial archive series)
    Collection of illustrations from the magazines Life and Judge.
    ISBN 0-486-41063-3 (pbk.)
        1. Caricatures and cartoons—United States. 2. American wit and humor, Pictorial.
I. Galewitz, Herb. II. Title. III. Series.

NC1426 .F5 2000
741.5'973'09042—dc21

                                                                        00-031398

Manufactured in the United States of America
Dover Publications, Inc., 31 East 2nd Street, Mineola, N.Y. 11501

Publisher's Note

At the beginning of the 20th century, *Judge* (established in 1881) and *Life* (1883), together with *Puck*, were the premier humor magazines in the United States. *Puck* disappeared in 1918, but, by the 1920s and early 30s, *Life* and *Judge* had achieved enormous popularity. Not until the establishment of the *New Yorker* in 1925 was their position seriously challenged.

This huge readership was due primarily to the magazines' cartoons. From politics to domestic bliss, childhood to boardroom, breadline to kick line—no subject was safe from the humorists' pens.

Not surprisingly, the promise of such a wide audience attracted some of the best artists in the country. Charles Dana Gibson, whose first published drawing appeared in *Life* in 1886, became *Life's* owner and editor in 1920. His finely detailed society drawings graced the magazine throughout the period, as did those of many of his imitators, including James Montgomery Flagg, best known as the artist who created the poster "Uncle Sam Wants You!" and Reginald Bathurst Birch, whose illustrations for Frances Hodgson Burnett's *Little Lord Fauntleroy* influenced a generation of boys' clothes. New artists introduced new subjects and styles: John Held, Jr. and Russell Patterson brought the flapper era to vivid life; A. B. Frost, the illustrator for Joel Chandler Harris' *Uncle Remus* books, introduced broad humor and slapstick to the cartoon; Rube Goldberg created crazy cartoon inventions that have become a synonym for complicated and impractical solutions; Art Young became the quintessential political cartoonist; and Dr. Seuss (Theodor Seuss Geisel) contributed comic creations that are immediately recognizable to those who know and love his children's books. These and other artists made *Life* and *Judge* an extraordinary visual archive of the 20s and 30s.

Sadly, the two magazines did not long survive the depression. The public, it seemed, was no longer in the mood to be entertained. *Life* ceased publication and sold its name to Time, Inc. in 1936. Although *Judge* continued to appear until the late 40s, it was but a shadow of its former self. Today, their richness can best be enjoyed in the pages of this lively collection of illustrations.

This rich source of copyright-free authentic 20s and 30s art can be used to give period flair to brochures, newsletters, advertisements, or any other graphic project.

Key to the Artists

The numbers under the illustrations refer to the artist, as listed below. The artists could not be identified for the illustrations on pages 118–123.

iv

Leatrice Joy

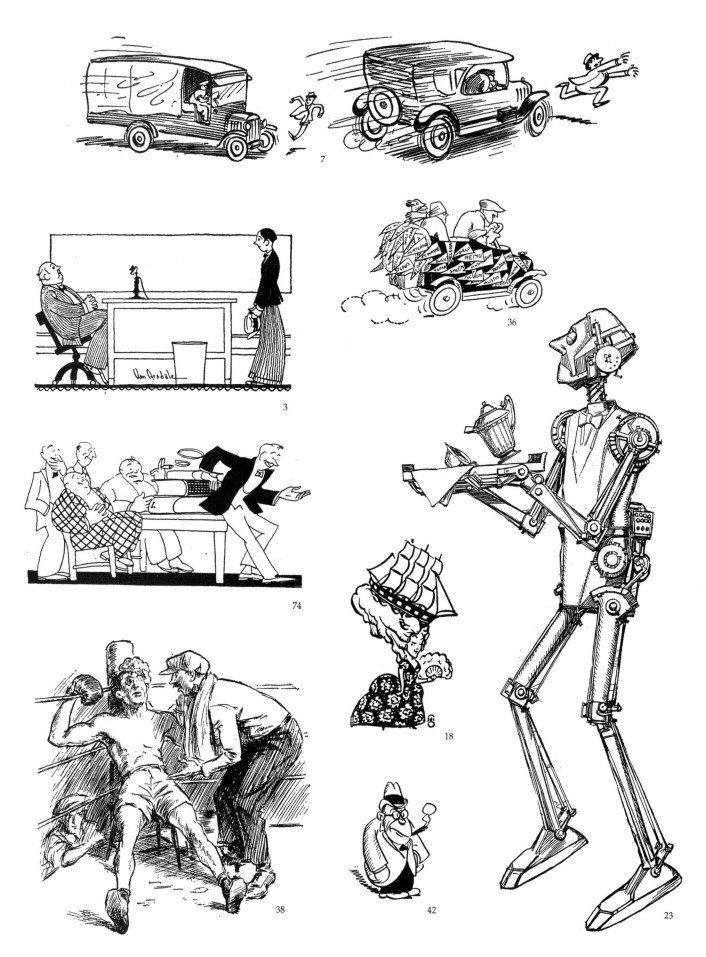

49

67

66

102

77

47

48

46

27

76

87

LOCKED
OUT
POKER PLAYER
NO. 62

FRED NEHER.

73

102

46

42

66

8

60

91

44

74

40

48

82

81

17

51

TICKETS

75

70

87

MILADY GLOVES

mulholland—

71

91

W N GROVE

43

66

j held jr

48

42

91

60

66

18

78

28

Mae McAvoy

75

63

13

"LINDY"

GOOD WILL

WANTED

FOR MURDER

33

91

48

103

18

80

79

66

42

14

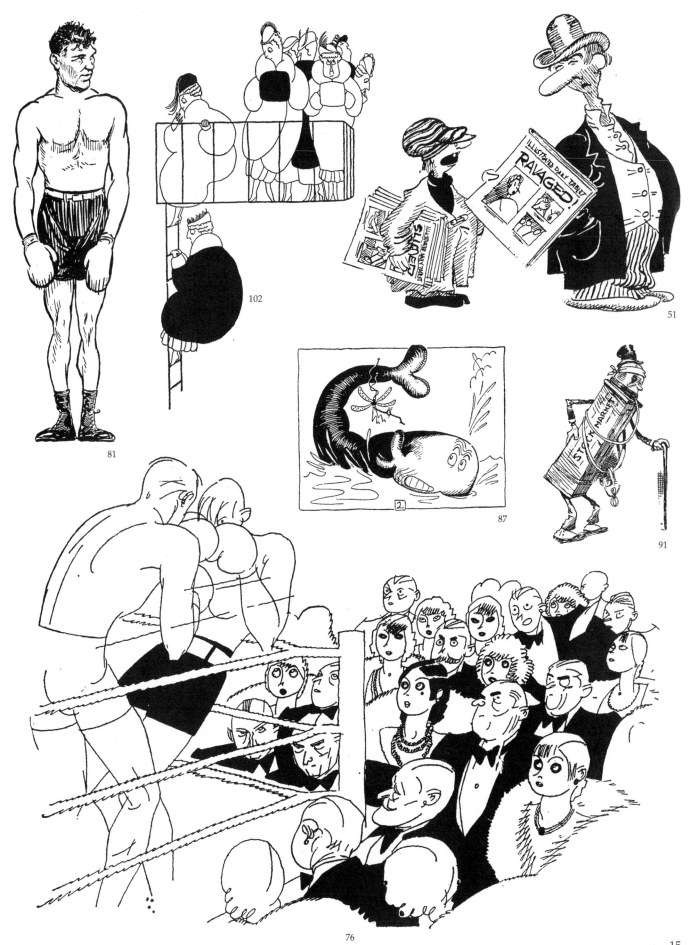

81

102

51

87

91

76

91

76

66

folks, meet professor bunQ!!

18

28

83

94

60

103

48

16

102

18

34

87

40

32

WOMEN! DO STRONG
MEN FIGHT OVER YOU?

Gloria Swanson

2

102

9

34

76

94

40

20

28

John Gilbert

66

94

33

61

CHEER UP,
MEN!
YOU CAN BE
JUST LIKE ME!

18

CARL
ANDERSON

48

31

1

8

76

66

48

42

103

33

22

87

18

81

94

FREE
SOUP

Thanksgiving Day 48

76

38

Jack Holt

28

john held jr 48

KODAK AS YOU GO

58

I.O.U.

58

POLICE PATROL

P.D

POLICE PATROL

94

81

CUCKOO!

58

42

76

40

26

64

32

85

86

102

51

33

MEN! BE MASTERFUL!

63

58

63

103

76

81

19

102

87

9

52

52

Barbara La Marr   28

57

8

35

48

51

54

52

92

40

10

34

42

54

33

18

16

YOU GAVE ME THE WRONG NUMBER AGAIN!

102

46

93

6

BASEBALL IS CROOKED

55

66

FOOD, JOBS, SHELTER

$

58

George Arliss

28

TAXI

81

81

81

40

18

102

Mae McAvoy   28

18

80

95

76

51

48

94

76

75

19

66

78

81

48

87

41

66

102

99

41

81

55

Adolphe Menjou

28

Jack Markow

98

40

81

43

33

11

95

103

18

45

76

48

102

86

81

87

19

66

45

66

86

48

99

34

95

46

40

102

herb
roth

33

87

19

32

76

48

95

7

48

86

Pedro de Cordoba

2

36

34

66

102

1

61

49

2

42

91

51

66

Buster Keaton   28

102

40

50

33

34

102

48

19

19

76

35

6

86

19

48

32

103

75

7

33

66

52

76

46

11

102

95

Lionel Barrymore

34

36

14

104

28

Norman Trevor

66

33

42

54

48

102

48

86

76

19

66

56

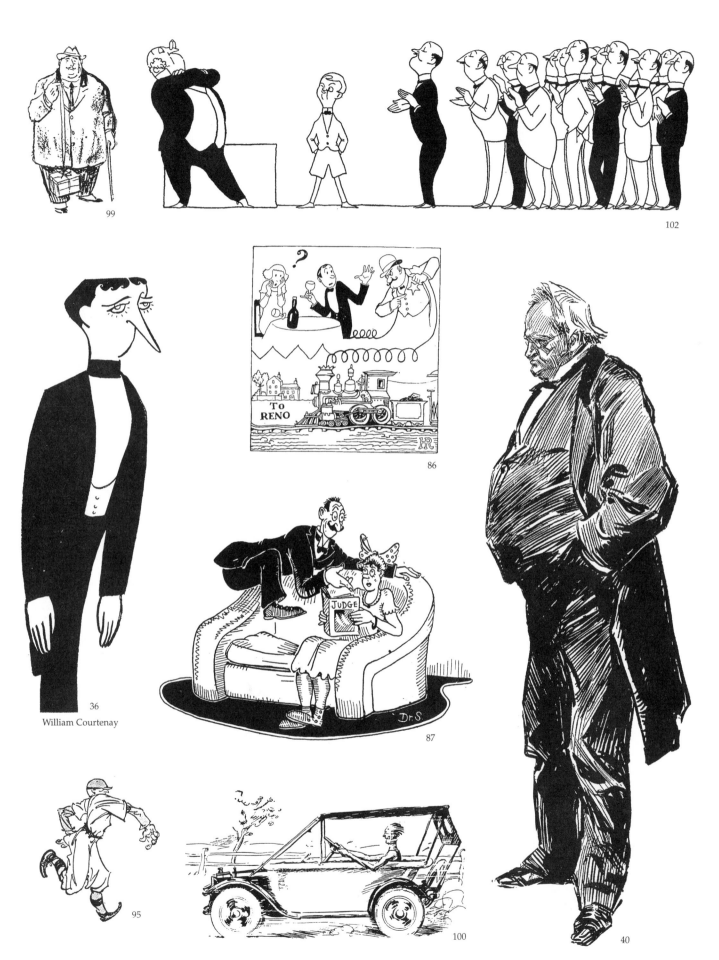

99

102

86

36

William Courtenay

87

95

100

40

81

32

66

51

57

86

96

48

SMUT SET
MAGAZINE
"SPICY — NOT RAW"

101

33

102

76

24

28

Douglas Fairbanks

40

81

33

104

100

60

11

76

32

80

29

102

55

18

19

66

37

61

53

Lenore Ulric

36

66

76

BARBER'S
STRIKE

42

102

48

28

Corinne Griffith

55

101

33

19

51

63

55

33

104

96

40

102

64

48

19

66

18

57

55

32

76

51

Balieff   36

48

33

66

19

76

7

48

102

2

81

42

90

1

28

Alfred Lunt

12

81

67

95

76

21

32

33

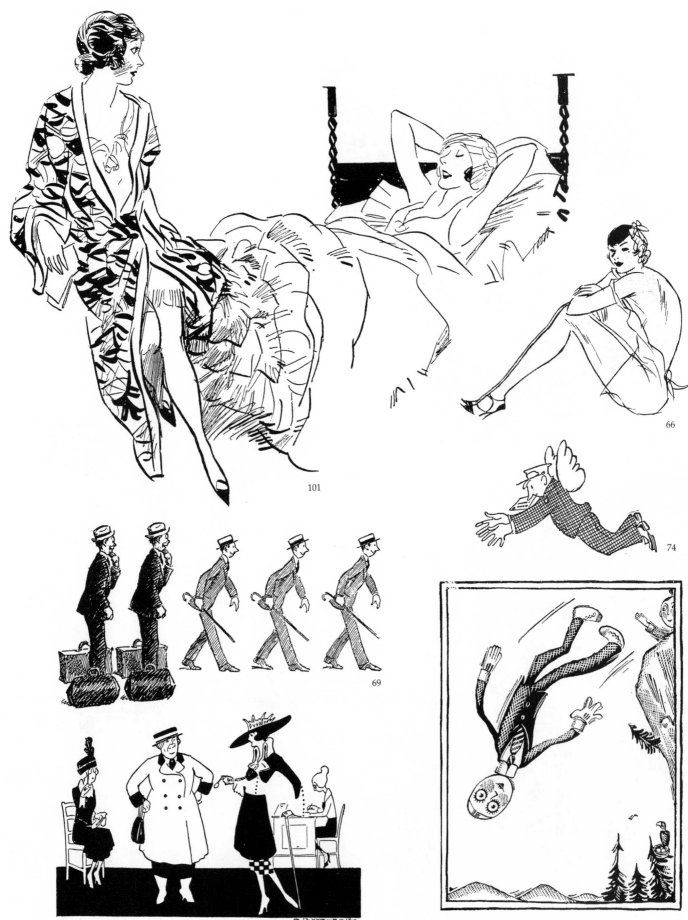

101

66

74

69

48

70

96

Adolphe Menjou

75

69

66

102

53

40

72

32

66

95

36

55

93

76

104

68

52

42

56

95

74

69

66

102

51

74

83

JAMES MONTGOMERY FLAGG

33

48

76

75

Alice Joyce

76

81

65

80

33

102

78

2

96

36

35

51

42

11

48

66

68

36

102

2

40

32

42

101

11

66

76

Lillian Gish 28

81

42

104

76

103

96

33

51

81

66

82

19

65

102

50

50

don herold

51

36

83

2

102

28

Margalo Gillmore

36

36

32

101

48

40

40

15

66

96

102

15

Buster Keaton

28

51

86

42

50

66

15

76

68

46

66

102

48

88

103

33

79

91

40

96

15

11

2

96

37

66

102

48

90

Next, Doctor

Say "Ah-h-h"

BOX OFFICE

Don Herold

51

76

36

78

70

51

8

32

86

42

66

76

40

77

92

28

Betty Bronson

18

15

32

96

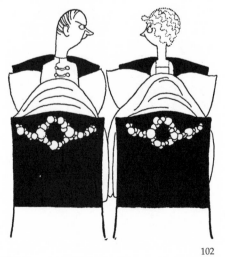

51

94

102

103

2

FIRST
PRIZE

53

76

11

77

26

95

37

77

46

18

25

40

102

48

J held jr

96

POIRET'S
SOIRÉES
SOIE

46

77

80

69

101

76

WHIRLING
DERVISH.

37

15

48

96

78

42

98

102

EDEN MUSEE

80

77

77

77

51

Don
Herold

102

58

57

46

40

96

75

4

7

7

66

15

46

37

50

15

102

102

59

NEW LINE OF LATEST FALL HATS MAZY'S STORE

DUNKEL

76

27

102

101

40

51

42

104

51

75

32

37

102

38

66

71

102

96

102

66

42

76

108

48

11

37

57

40

37

78

22

58

57

48

96

48

102

66

57

110

111

102

50

66

JUDGE JR'S NIGHT GUIDE

66

77

32

78

37

40

75

97

81

75

78

51

102

2

8

48

42

57

32

48

87

75

102

69

75

50

102

58

54

CONSTRUCTION
OF THE
BRIDGE
HERE
WILL START IN
OCTOBER

38

52

99

42

AMERICAN
BAR

SEE THE MOON 10¢

53

102

75

116

37

102

42

41

42

40

R.B.FULLER

37

51

48